Jazz Guitar Duets
Etudes on Familiar Chord Progressions for Two Guitars

By Tim Fischer and William Flynn

Online Audio

To Access the Online Audio Go to:
www.melbay.com/30558MEB

Acknowledgments

The authors wish to thank Frank Potenza, Nick Stoubis, and Mel Bay Publishing for their support of this project. Additional thanks go to those who read and played through multiple rough drafts, providing helpful feedback and editorial suggestions along the way: Dennis Hodges, Chris Motter, Peter Block, and the Wichita State University guitar studio. Lastly, thanks to Louis Michael at Lewis and Clark Community College, who graciously provided a space for the authors to record the accompanying audio tracks.

Audio Tracks

New Blue
1. Full Etude
2. Gtr 1
3. Gtr 2

Prince's Waltz
4. Full Etude
5. Gtr 1
6. Gtr 2

Minor Blues in G
7. Full Etude
8. Gtr 1
9. Gtr 2

Two of You
10. Full Etude
11. Gtr 1
12. Gtr 2

Major Blues in F
13. Full Etude
14. Gtr 1
15. Gtr 2

Rhythm Squabble
16. Full Etude
17. Gtr 1
18. Gtr 2

All Your Things
19. Full Etude
20. Gtr 1
21. Gtr 2

Why So Blue, Alice?
22. Full Etude
23. Gtr 1
24. Gtr 2

Dawn
25. Full Etude
26. Gtr 1
27. Gtr 2

Lester Stomps In
28. Full Etude
29. Gtr 1
30. Gtr 2

Table of Contents

Introduction

It is safe to say that guitarists are a unique bunch. Guitarists congregate together, perform together, share ideas together, and practice together. It is maybe because of this affinity for socializing that guitar duos are so prevalent. It may also be that the dual ability of the guitar to perform melody and accompaniment allows for mimicking an entire ensemble in the absence of other instruments. This ability is matched in the Western world only by the piano, but the portability of the guitar has allowed for guitar duos to become more common; whether it be a club, cafe, or a street corner, guitar duos perform in places where the space for two pianos simply isn't available.

In jazz music, guitar duos stretch back to the first stylistic era in the late 1920s recordings of Eddie Lang and Lonnie Johnson (*Blue Guitars*), with other famous jazz guitar duos being Carl Kress and Dick McDonough (*Pioneers of Jazz Guitar*), Chuck Wayne and Joe Puma (*Interactions*), Joe Pass and Herb Ellis (*Two for the Road*), John Abercrombie and Ralph Towner (*Sargasso Sea*), and Jim Hall and Pat Metheny (*Jim Hall & Pat Metheny*). This book was written to provide music for two guitars in the jazz style, embracing the communal aspects of the instrument. By providing original music created with the sole intention of being performed by two guitars, the entire range of each instrument can be explored. Through counterpoint, harmony, bass lines, cross rhythms, and quick swaps of roles, each etude is intended to showcase a different possibility of two guitars performing together outside of the traditional melody and chord functions.

If the popularity of two guitars performing together is unique to the instrument, so then too is the common lack of reading skills most guitars possess compared to other instrumentalists. Partly due to the folk nature of the instrument, many guitarists get their start performing music by ear or by watching other guitarists, rarely learning music through standard notation. We believe that guitarists interested in improving their sight-reading skills are more likely to accomplish this goal by tapping into the communal aspect at the core of the instrument, as well as performing music that is exciting and intellectually stimulating. *Jazz Guitar Duets* aims to assist guitarists in improving their sight-reading skills through duo performance.

How to Use This Book

Book Organization

As you move through the book, you will find that the etudes increase in level of difficulty. Each etude is preceded by a thorough analysis that details its essential musical characteristics and harmonic progression, as well as offers suggestions regarding ways to apply those ideas to the reader's own improvisations and compositions. Some of the terms used in the analysis section may not be familiar to the reader. We suggest examining popular jazz theory books or free internet resources to help define any unknown musical term.

Along with the score and analysis, there are three different recordings for each etude:

- Recording of etude with both Guitar 1 and Guitar 2
- Recording of etude with isolated Guitar 1
- Recording of etude with isolated Guitar 2

Sight-Reading

Read through both Guitar 1 and Guitar 2 in each of the ten etudes to help improve your sight-reading skills. Keep in mind that while many guitarists start by learning to sight-read in the open position, open strings can "stick out" in timbre against fretted notes. Examine the general range of the part before reading, and if it falls mostly within and slightly above the staff, consider starting at the fifth position. This will allow access to two ledger lines both above and below the staff. Once you are comfortable playing the etude in fifth position, play through the same etude in another position to challenge your fretboard understanding. Keep in mind that we guitar players are not often granted the convenience of being able to play an entire melody strictly in one position. Therefore, shifting between positions is inevitable. When necessary, these shifts should occur in ways that best support the musical phrase, and they should always be made as inaudible as possible. Additionally, be sure to relate the written melodies to both the key center and the chord symbols. This will encourage processing the etude in real time and allow you to better interpret the notes in groups, similar to how we process written language. Also, understand that the etudes in this book are written for guitar. Therefore, they do not need to be transposed up an octave.

Sight-reading the melodies in conjunction with the accompanying audio recordings will greatly enhance the sight-reading benefits of this book. Use the recordings to either play a part in unison with the recording to check your rhythm and note accuracy, or play one of the guitar parts against the opposite part to create a "virtual" duet. Playing one part against the accompaniment is especially challenging when an etude features two parts with independent rhythms. The tempos indicated on the score are used for each of the recordings and merely function as a suggested goal. Find a tempo that allows for reading the music without stopping and, from there, increase the tempo as you get more comfortable with the music. Many of the etudes continue to work past the given tempo markings, so feel free to experiment!

Studying Jazz Vocabulary

The musical vocabulary of improvised jazz is a stylistic language comparable to a spoken language. We learn a second language (taking a foreign language class in high school, for example) by studying the grammar, syntax, and vocabulary of the language, all while listening to and imitating examples of the language being spoken. Similarly, our path to learning the jazz language is filled not only with studying the theory behind the music: the chords, scales, arpeggios, melodic gestures, and applications thereof; but also (and more importantly), listening to, playing with, and imitating other jazz musicians by either playing with them live or on recordings. Use the following etudes to come to a better understanding of the jazz language through detailed analysis and study as well as by listening to the recordings while reading the scores.

Reharmonization and Chord Substitution

All the etudes in this book are based on the chords to popular jazz standards. The harmonic progressions of these standards offer countless opportunities for reharmonization and chord substitutions. Several of these principles are illustrated in these etudes. Find lead sheets for the songs that these etudes are based on, and study the etude progressions side-by-side with the "standard" sets of changes. Come to a theoretical understanding of how and why the substitutions work. It is important to understand that jazz musicians improvise not only with a song's melody and rhythm, but also with a song's harmony. Developing a repertoire of common reharmonization techniques employed on these standards will help familiarize your ears with hearing variations to jazz progressions, which will in turn prepare you to recognize them on the bandstand and react appropriately.

Articulation, Phrasing, and Time Feel

When performing written jazz music, much of the performance details are left "off the page." Use the recordings as a tool to better understand how to turn the written notes and rhythms into music that sounds and feels like jazz. Pay particular attention to when notes are played long versus short and the dynamic shape of the musical phrases. In longer musical ideas, specific notes are accented and are an important aspect of the swing style. Hearing these jazz melodies played without rhythm section accompaniment can allow the listener to pick up on more nuanced articulations than is sometimes possible when listening to an instrument performing with a full ensemble.

Accompaniment

As instrumentalists capable of playing both melodies and harmonies, the role of accompanying others is incredibly important. Work through the chords of each etude and practice comping along to the Guitar 1 tracks. Be sure to practice different rhythmic styles and approaches, as well as different voicing types. For the swing etudes, practice both "Freddie Green"-style rhythm guitar (i.e. two- and three-note voicings on the bottom strings, played in quarter notes) and bebop-style comping (i.e. free rhythms and voicing types, balancing long and short durations with an emphasis on filling-in melodic gaps). Use the etude "New Blue" as an opportunity to practice bossa nova accompaniment patterns, or "Prince's Waltz" to work on accompaniment in a more modern, straight-eighth note style.

Two-Line Jazz Harmonization

For those interested in writing their own etudes, study each guitar part, noting the following musical elements: register of parts, composite pitches against the given chord symbol, harmonic intervals between parts (especially in relation to on and off the beat), melodic direction of parts, rhythmic independence of parts, and melodic and rhythmic imitation between parts. There are no steadfast rules when writing duets, so take inspiration from all musical styles.

We hope you enjoy the music contained in this book and find it worthwhile in your musical studies, whatever they might be!

Etudes

This page has been left bank
to avoid awkward page turns.

New Blue

Key Concepts

- Outlining chords with arpeggios
- Dorian scale over tonic minor chords
- Phrygian Dominant scale over minor ii-Vs
- Transposed motifs
- Chromatic passing tones

Each chorus of this etude begins with arpeggios outlining the chord changes (mm. 1-4 and mm. 17-19). Note that in mm. 1, 3, & 17-18, upper-structure arpeggios (E♭maj7 over Cmin7, and A♭maj7 over Fmin7) are used to achieve 9th chord colors. The tonic Cmin7 chords in this etude are treated with distinct Dorian colors as opposed to melodic minor colors, which is a characteristic of post-modal jazz composition. Another scale choice to observe is the use of the G Phrygian Dominant scale (5th mode C harmonic minor) over the Dmin7(♭5) and G7(♭9) chords. This scale is a common choice for describing a ii-V progression in a minor key.

Another technique this etude demonstrates is using a transposed motif to outline two different chords (mm. 5-6). The motif in m. 5, which highlights the ♭5, 11, and ♭3 of the Dmin7(♭5) chord, is transposed up a minor third to the G7(♭9) chord where it highlights the 3, ♯9, and ♭9.

Lastly, note the use of chromatic neighbor and passing tones in this etude. There are no strict rules governing the use of these tones in jazz, but they will typically sound best when used to resolve and draw attention to the strong notes of a chord's triad. Oftentimes, as in m. 28, the chromatic passing and neighbor tones are occurring on offbeats, and the strong notes they resolve to are occurring on downbeats.

New Blue

Straight ♩ = 110

Fischer/Flynn

10

This page has been left bank
to avoid awkward page turns.

Prince's Waltz

Key Concepts

- Accented chromatic neighbor tones
- Reharmonization
- Rhythmic hemiolas
- Two-part call and response

The melody of Guitar 1 in "Prince's Waltz" takes its inspiration from the melody of the tune on which this etude is based. Where the original melody uses non-chord tones pulling down by step to create tension, the melody of "Prince's Waltz" approaches chord tones from below. The tension created by non-chord tone melodies can be increased by placing the chromatic pitches on the strong part of the beat in what is often referred to as "accented non-chord tone." See mm. 1-4, and 8 for specific examples of this device. The use of accented, chromatic non-chord tones, along with the straight-eighth note pulse helps give this etude a more classical flavor.

Two chords of the standard progression are reharmonized in "Prince's Waltz." At mm. 6 and 22, the more common G7 is replaced with the tritone substitute D♭7 in an attempt to present a new harmonic color. This stands in contrast to the G7 harmony that occurs two measures prior. In m. 18, the D7 chord is replaced with E7. This change in harmony on the second A section helps convey a difference between the two A sections and was used by the pianist Bill Evans in live performances of the original tune.

The individual guitar parts in this etude are designed to create a call-and-response pattern, with each part taking on a more active rhythmic role during the sustained or rest sections of the other part. This independence in rhythms provides a great performance challenge. Make sure to keep an internal sense of the 3/4 meter when reading your part with your duet partner or the accompanying recording. This rhythmic independence is not completely broken until mm. 25-27, when both parts suggest a two-beat, repeating *hemiola* against the underlying meter of three (for another example of hemiola, see "Major Blues in F"). The accent marks above the melody in these measures help outline the beginning of each two-beat figure. The piece ends with a brief one-measure, deceptive cadence built on the ♭II chord and is inspired by Freddie Hubbard's famous waltz that is also in B♭.

Prince's Waltz

Fischer/Flynn

Straight ♩ = 115

This page has been left bank
to avoid awkward page turns.

Minor Blues in G

Key Concepts
- Melodic minor scale on tonic minor chords
- Substituting for a V/iv chord in the 4th bar of a minor blues
- Tritone substitution in a minor ii-V
- minMaj7 arpeggio over a 7#11 chord
- Diminished 7 arpeggios

Unlike "New Blue," "Minor Blues in G" uses distinct melodic minor colors for the tonic minor chords. For example, note the clear use of the G melodic minor scale in both Guitars 1 and 2 on the Gmin6 chord in mm. 7-8. This etude also features a common chord substitution found in a minor blues, which involves turning the i chord into a dominant chord in m. 4 of the progression, changing the function of the chord from a i to a V7/iv. Over these measures (mm. 4, 16, 28), note the use of the G Phrygian Dominant scale.

Another common area for harmonic variation in a minor blues is m. 9 of the progression. The following three chords all commonly occur at this point in the form: iimin7(♭5) (Amin7(♭5)), V/V (A7), and a tritone substitute for V/V (E♭7). This etude uses the last option, which can be observed in mm. 9, 21, and 33. Notice how the chord symbol contains a #11 extension. The #11 over an E♭7 is the note A, and helps reinforce the fact that this chord is substituting for an A7. An oft-used scale over a 7#11 chord is the Lydian Dominant scale (R, 2, 3, #4, 5, 6, ♭7), which is the fourth mode of the melodic minor scale. In this case, the E♭ Lydian Dominant scale is the fourth mode of the B♭ melodic minor scale. Note the use of this scale over the E♭7#11 in mm. 9, 21, and 33. In m. 9, a B♭minMaj9 arpeggio is used.

Another arpeggio concept featured in this etude is using a dim7 arpeggio to elicit a 7(♭9) sound over a dominant 7 chord (mm. 4, 14, 16, 28). Due to the symmetrical nature of a dim7 arpeggio (it is constructed entirely in minor third intervals), it can be built off the 3, 5, 7, or ♭9 of a dominant 7 chord and will still contain the same notes. This is not only an effective way to define an altered dominant, but can also be used to play over the entirety of a minor ii-V progression (as seen in m. 14).

Minor Blues in G

Swing ♩ = 120

Fischer/Flynn

This page has been left bank
to avoid awkward page turns.

Two of You

Key Concepts
- Subdividing and counting rests through highly-syncopated rhythms
- Tritone ii-V substitution
- Chromatic ii-V substitution
- Lydian Dominant colors (9, ♯11, 13 on dominant 7 chord)

The defining musical characteristic of "Two of You" is space. The A sections (mm. 1-8 & 17-24) of this etude feature an extremely syncopated and sparse melody in Guitar 1 that is harmonized with the same rhythm in Guitar 2. When playing a piece of music that contains this much syncopation and space, be sure to do two things: 1) actively count through the rests, and 2) subdivide the quarter-note pulse. Counting through the rests will help you stay focused when not actively playing your instrument and will help eliminate the guess work of your next entrance. As far as subdividing with slower tempos like this, it is helpful to think of the eighth-note subdivision (think "1 & 2 & 3 & 4 &"). At very slow swing tempos it is best to think of the triplet subdivision, and at very fast swing tempos to think of larger divisions such as half notes or whole notes.

There are two interesting chord substitutions in this etude worth discussing, the first of which occurs in m. 8. The chord that typically occurs here is an E♭7. However, in this etude the E♭7 is substituted with a dominant 7th chord whose root is a tritone away: A7. The A7 is then preceded with its corresponding ii chord to create a ii-V progression in the key of D. The V7 chord (A7) in this substitute chord progression resolves smoothly by half step to the next chord: A♭maj7. This type of chord substitution is often referred to as a "tritone ii-V progression" and can be easily implemented in a ii-V progression in which the ii and V chords each last for one measure. The second interesting chord substitution in this etude occurs in m. 15-16. The progression to the original tune typically contains an Fmin7 in m. 15 and B♭7 in m. 16. The substitution used in this etude condenses the ii-V into m. 16 and precedes it with a ii-V a half-step higher in m. 15.

Like "Minor Blues In G," "Two of You" features a clear use of the Lydian Dominant scale. Mm. 13-14 in the etude contain a V/V chord (F9♯11), which is a commonly-occurring chord in standard jazz progressions, and is an ideal harmony over which to use this scale. Notice how Guitar 1 in mm. 13-14 is arpeggiating an E♭maj7(♯5). The notes of this arpeggio (E♭, G, B, D) highlight the ♭7, 9, ♯11, and 13 of the F9♯11 chord.

Two of You

Fischer/Flynn

This page has been left bank
to avoid awkward page turns.

Major Blues in F

Key Concepts
- Bebop melodic vocabulary
- Chord variations and substitutions
- Rhythmic hemiolas
- Turnarounds

There are many ways to enhance the staple twelve-bar blues chord progression. Some reharmonized progressions are common enough that they take on a new name amongst musicians (see "Why So Blue, Alice?" for such an example). Common areas in the twelve-bar progression that are updated include movement from I to IV, leaving the IV to return back to I or a related substitute, the replacement of the typical last four measures of the form with a modified ii-V, and varying the turnaround progression to return to the top of the form. In this etude, tritone substitutes are used for a stronger pull to the IV chord (m. 28), in the typical ii-V-I (m. 34), and on the turnaround in mm. 23-24. In mm. 18 and 30, a iv replaces the common ♯IV diminished chord.

Substitute harmony, when stated melodically, is only effective if the harmony can be convincingly outlined and creatively used in the context of the standard chord progression. Bebop melodic vocabulary helped solidify the art of chord outlining in jazz improvisation, creating interesting melodies and rhythms, all the while outlining common and substitute harmony. Many of the eighth-note lines in this etude are based on bebop melodic practices, dictating what chord tones, extensions, and chromatic notes fall on and off the beat. The harmony of the twelve-bar progression should still be audible even when the Guitar 1 part is played alone. When listening to the accompanying recordings, pay particular attention to which notes in the eighth-note lines are accented compared to which notes are "ghosted," or are barely audible. The dynamic contour is just as important as the note choice when performing bebop-style eighth-note melodies.

Smaller melodic motives are provided extra life by making slight alterations in order to fit changes in the underlying harmony. See mm. 25-28, 29-32, and 33-34 for different examples of this technique. To help provide some "macro" direction to longer eighth-note phrases, important chromatic sequences are hidden in the middle of melodic phrases. Mm. 1-3 suggest a rising chromatic melody of A-B♭-B-C in half notes starting on beat three, while mm. 13-15 are based on a descending chromatic melody of A-A♭-G-G♭ (the resolving F occurs two measures later, in m. 17, as the lowest point of the melody before the end of the phrase). In addition to this chromatic, descending guide tone, mm. 13-15 feature a three-beat, repeating rhythmic cell, temporarily hiding the underling meter. This hemiola occurs four times before returning to the beat one of m. 16. Triplets and sixteenth notes are used in several places to help break up the constant stream of eighth notes. These rhythmic "excite" points are each performed according to jazz swing practices and left-hand slurring; if you are unfamiliar with the specific execution, be sure to listen to the accompanying recording.

Major Blues in F

Swing ♩ = 135

Fischer/Flynn

Rhythm Squabble

Key Concepts

* Melodies over "quick" harmonic rhythm
* Guide tone eighth-note lines
* Bebop melodic vocabulary
* Tritone substitutes
* Two-part call and response

Tension is created in "Rhythm Squabble" by creating a call-and-response dialogue between the two guitar parts. The roles of melody and accompaniment are switched between the eight-measure A sections. At the beginning of the bridge, the rate of change of melodic roles is increased to every two measures. The tension is resolved when the parts come together in rhythmic unison at the end of the bridge. While the roles of each part should be clear based on range and melodic density, listening to the accompanying recording will help further clarify which melodies should receive louder dynamics and which melodies should be played at a lower, accompaniment-like volume.

One of the challenges of improvising on a "rhythm changes" chord progression (the common name given to songs based on the chords to Gershwin's classic tune) is the quick harmonic rhythm. Much of the harmonic rhythm is based on two-beat units, meaning that the fewer notes used in a melody to suggest the underlying harmony, the better. Reference the pitches of each part with the provided chord symbols. Notes that are not common in adjacent chords can be used to great effect when telling the listener of a new harmony. There is also a great deal of emphasis placed on the *guide-tones* (the third and seventh) of each harmony and the step-wise movement of these pitches through this and other common jazz harmonic progressions.

The B section of "Rhythm Squabble" provides a much needed contrast to the quick harmonic rhythm of the A sections. To help provide a little more harmonic motion than the typical two-measure dominant seventh chords, a minor seventh chord precedes each of the dominant seventh chords, making each a ii-V progression. On the next page is the typical "rhythm changes" bridge and the modified bridge used as a starting point for "Rhythm Squabble."

This series of "ii-V"s is modified one step further. Mm. 19-20 replace the Dmin7-G7 with the tritone substitute of G7, Db7 and its related ii-7 chord (see "Two of You" for another example of this device). This substitute creates a descending chromatic progression and should be viewed as one of many possibilities for embellishing the bridge in a rhythm changes song.

TYPICAL BRIDGE

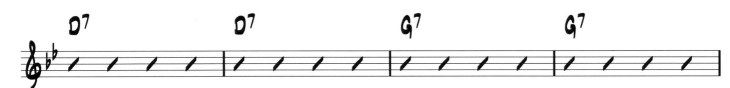

MODIFIED BRIDGE WITH II-Vs

MODIFIED BRIDGE WITH TRITONE II-Vs

Rhythm Squabble

Swing ♩ = 120

Fischer/Flynn

This page has been left bank
to avoid awkward page turns.

All Your Things

Key Concepts
- The first A section is transposed up a fifth for the second A section
- Reading low ledger-lines in Guitar 2
- Constructing melodies with guide tones
- 1-2-3-5 patterns

In this etude, notice how the second A section (mm. 9-16) is the same as the first (mm. 1-8), only transposed up a perfect fifth. In the Guitar 1 part, try beginning the first A section in V position and the second A section in VIII position. If you are one of the many guitarists that struggle with reading ledger lines, pay special attention to the Guitar 2 part, specifically during the bridge (rehearsal letter B).

This progression is an ideal study for connecting 3rds and 7ths between chords. Mm. 29-31 illustrate an excellent way of using these guide tones to build a line. M. 29 begins on the 3 of D♭maj7, then uses a three-note cell to resolve down a half step to the 7 of G♭7 in m. 30. After the resolution in m. 30, the line uses a similar three-note cell to resolve down another half step to the 3 of the Cmin7 in m. 31. These 3-7-3 connections happen throughout the entirety of this progression and are great source material for constructing and connecting lines (see "Rhythm Squabble" for another example of this device).

Another common idea this etude demonstrates is found on beats three and four of m. 24, and is a melodic device often used over altered dominant chords. This four-note pattern descends through the 5, 3, 2, and Root of C♯/D♭ minor. Patterns like these are often referred to as "1-2-3-5 patterns," and they are extremely useful and versatile patterns to use in improvising. Here, the pattern is being used to highlight the ♯5, 3, ♯9, and ♭9 of the C7(♯5) chord.

All Your Things

Swing ♩ = 107

Fischer/Flynn

36

Why So Blue, Alice?

Key Concepts
- Reading ledger lines
- 1-2-3-5 patterns
- Constructing melodies with guide tones
- Using 7-3 resolutions
- Embellishing triads

Similar to "All Your Things," "Why So Blue, Alice?" requires a good deal of reading ledger lines in the upper and lower registers. In Guitar 1, pay close attention to rehearsal letter C, which spends most of its time above the staff. The Guitar 2 part is fairly low throughout, especially the very beginning (mm. 1-4).

This etude illustrates two more concepts found in "All Your Things." First, notice the use of 1-2-3-5 patterns in mm. 16-20. These were introduced in one application in m. 24 of "All Your Things," and are introduced in two other applications here. The descending minor 1-2-3-5 pattern in the second half of m. 16 is built a half-step above the F7 chord and highlights the chord's ♯5, 3, ♯9, and ♭9. In m. 17, a major 1-2-3-5 pattern is built on the 5 of the B♭maj7 chord. This application highlights the 5, 6, 7, and 9 of the chord. Mm. 18-19 and the first half of m. 20 all use minor 1-2-3-5 patterns built off the root of the ii chord in each bar.

The other concept in this etude that was introduced in "All Your Things" is using guide tones as a basis for constructing melodies. This can be seen in mm. 29-31 of "Why So Blue, Alice?" in that each measure is connected with a chromatically descending quarter note on the downbeat. This chromatic line traces the resolutions of the 3 of B♭maj7, 3 of B♭min7, and 3 of Amin7. In a "Bird blues" progression (a common name for this blues reharmonization, coined after the nickname of bebop architect Charlie Parker), this chromatically descending line could potentially be continued into m. 32 with a C♭ (the 3 of A♭min7), and then to m. 33 with a B♭ (the 3 of Gmin7).

Another passage of guide tone connection occurs in mm. 7-9. Rather than connecting 3rds, however, the lines are resolving the 7 to 3 between the ii and V chords. The half-step resolution from the 7 of the ii chord to the 3 of the V chord is the strongest resolution found in the ii-V progression, and mastery of it is an important and necessary step in gaining an authentic command of bebop vocabulary.

Triad embellishment is another melodic device commonly found in bebop vocabulary. M. 25 illustrates a typical way of embellishing a major triad. Notice the way the jagged line uses diatonic upper and lower neighbor tones to surround the notes of an F major triad. Study this pattern and practice applying it to other major (and minor) triads in all keys.

Why So Blue, Alice?

Swing ♩ = 110

Fischer/Flynn

This page has been left bank
to avoid awkward page turns.

Dawn

Key Concepts

- Altered harmony on dominant seventh chords
- Melodic minor colors on tonic minor chords
- Rhythmic displacement with triplets
- Asymmetrical diminished scale patterns
- Chord voicings

The etude "Dawn" is loosely inspired by the cool-school approach of alto saxophonist Lee Konitz. Konitz was an early student of the pianist Lennie Tristano and, along with Tristano's other students, wrote original melodies over the chord progressions of jazz standards. The "brighter" color provided by the melodic minor scale's raised 6 and 7 scale degrees (A and B) helps provide a stronger contrast to the altered tensions (♭9, ♯9, ♭5) on the V7 chord (A♭, B♭, and D♭). The descending chromatic melody of E♭, D, D♭, and C during mm. 1-3 is emphasized by being placed on downbeats. This descending melody is answered by an ascending melody of E♭, F, G, A♭, G in mm. 5-7.

The bridge begins with a repeating, two-note cell that shifts emphasis on each note through a change in rhythm. This common, swing-era device helps the improviser get more mileage out of fewer notes. It is immediately followed by a phrase of larger intervals (mm. 13-14) over the Edim7. The melodic content on this chord comes from the E diminished scale (whole-half) and continues the focus on interesting rhythms by accenting unconventional points in the triplet subdivision.

After a return to the A section, the end of the piece features contrary motion (one part ascends while the other descends), and is capped off with two common minMaj7 chord voicings that are spread over two octaves. The minMaj7 chord, with an added 9 (see Guitar 1), is a popular ending harmony for a minor key song.

Dawn

Swing ♩ = 125

Fischer/Flynn

This page has been left bank
to avoid awkward page turns.

Lester Stomps In

Key Concepts

- Two-part call and response
- Swing-era riff accompaniment
- Chromatic passing tones and enclosures
- Guide tone accompaniment
- Rhythmic displacement with triplets

"Lester Stomps In," as the name implies, is an ode to the great, swing-era saxophonist Lester Young. Young's ability to improvise simple, repeating "riffs" to provide accompaniment behind soloists of the Count Basie Orchestra is well-documented. With this idea in mind, Guitar 2 is written to demonstrate Young-like riffs in between the melody of Guitar 1. The notes of this accompaniment change along with the harmonic progression, and demonstrate guide tone accompaniment during the ii-V-I progression in mm. 5-7. Guitar 2 clearly outlines the turnaround at the end of the first A section (mm. 7-8) by using the notes of the harmony and smoothly leading in and out of notes not found in the home key of D♭ (D♮, A♮). This same principle is found in mm. 4, 12, and 28, over the B♭7(♭9) chord with the notes D♮ and B♮.

Melody and accompaniment roles are switched during the bridge (see "Rhythm Squabble" for another etude that switches roles between the parts). Guitar 1 plays a simple half-note melody while Guitar 2 shifts to bebop-style eighth-note lines. The eighth notes turn into triplets in mm. 20-22, where a pattern of four (indicated by accent marks) further highlights the rhythmic dissonance against the underlying pulse. When playing this rhythmic idea, it will prove helpful to hear the accompanying half notes in Guitar 1 as an indicator of the pulse.

Lester Stomps In

Swing ♩ = 140

Fischer/Flynn

New Blue
with position markings

Straight ♩ = 110

Fischer/Flynn

Minor Blues in G

with position markings

Fischer/Flynn

About The Authors

Tim Fischer

Growing up in Los Angeles, Tim had the good fortune to study and perform with many of the great musicians that call the city home. The lessons learned during his formative years in Los Angeles are compiled on his debut album as a leader, *Due South*, an album that features his original compositions and arrangements performed by a mix of friends from both the West Coast and Midwest. Recordings featuring Tim's work as a sideman demonstrate the versatility of his approach to improvisational music, encompassing straight-ahead archtop tones (Alex Smith Trio), neo-classical acoustic guitar work (Cinematic Guitar Ensemble), and distortion pedal riffing (Michael Mull Octet). He has performed across the United States as well as in Europe.

Tim is active in jazz education, having presented his research on the Miles Davis first quintet at Northwestern University, University of Southern California, California Institute of the Arts, Eastern Washington University, Pasadena City College, and the Seattle Jazz Guitar Society. He has worked as an adjudicator for the Lionel Hampton Jazz Festival and instructor of combos and big bands for the Monterey Jazz Festival's Summer Jazz Camp. An experienced computer programmer, Tim has also presented clinics on website development and online marketing for the music and design schools at California Institute of the Arts. Tim begins an appointment as Assistant Professor of Music at Coastal Carolina University in the fall of 2016 and holds a doctorate in music from the University of Southern California.

www.timfischermusic.com

William Flynn

William Flynn is a Kansas-based jazz guitarist and composer whose playing has been praised as "uplifting and inspiring" (F5 Magazine), and is described as "playing a mean guitar" (Wichita Eagle). William is a first-call guitarist in the Wichita area, regularly appearing as both a leader and sideman at local clubs and festivals. Equally accomplished and respected as an educator, William has taught and presented at conferences, universities, and societies around the country.

William holds a Bachelor of Music degree in Jazz Studies from Capital University (Columbus, OH), and a Master of Music degree from the University of North Texas, where he held a position as Graduate Teaching Fellow. As a member of the One O' Clock Lab Band, he can be heard on *Lab 2012*. William's most recent release as a leader, *The Songbook Project*, is available on the Armored Records label.

William currently serves as Assistant Professor of Jazz Guitar at Wichita State University, where he teaches applied jazz guitar, jazz improvisation, and directs the Guitar Ensemble.

www.williamflynnmusic.com